Stories Of A Woman

Her Leap In Faith

Shweta Lanke- Kane

BookLeaf Publishing

India | USA | UK

Made with ❤ on the BookLeaf Publishing Platform
www.bookleafpub.in
www.bookleafpub.com

Dedication

With gratitude and humility,
I remember every person I met,
And every experience I had.
I dedicate every word herein to the Universe,
Who has been my guiding star,
Form since to ever.

Preface

I met few women of inspiration,
And read about some,
They helped me to take a leap in life.
The only motivation is to express myself,
Tell stories of opportunities, adventures and learnings,
Along with of heartbreaks, agony and failures.
Life happens,
As we learn from each experience, experiment and
encounter,
Everything make sense at the end.

Acknowledgements

I am grateful to my father-in-law,
Who wanted me to pen my experiences of working far
from home.
He believed if one woman is motivated to take a leap,
Shedding her fears and boundaries,
And walk into this world with valour and dignity,
It's worth it.
This is my first attempt,
And I have a long way to go.
There's much more to comprehend,
Before I rest for one last time.

And Vinod Kumar Wuthoo Sir,
Who believed I can write far before I even realised.

1. Love is in Search of Closure

Unaware, I was trapped by memories from the past,
My yester years from nowhere glanced at me,
I, now-a-days, prefer hiding behind my todays,
So as to not to confront each other anymore.
I couldn't see those demons coming,
Hence, had no time to hold my shield high,
They caught me vulnerable,
But I decided to sit with them today.
Thoughts aimlessly appeared and disappeared,
Leaving me clueless of their beginnings and endings,
I looked at the book on my window plane,
And mirrored myself to those pages randomly blown by
the wind.
And then, all of a sudden, I lost my heart beat,
I smelled you in the fragrance of those dried petals,
Kept in between the pages of my forever favourite book,
I remembered our short-lived love story that fills my
heart even today.
My gut crammed and here's my sinking heart,
Long lost love was right in front of me,
Bringing back everything that I buried deep down in my
core,
I couldn't help but to sit and watch what I hesitated to

even think.

My lips still shiver when your kisses cross my mind,

Laying closely beside each other, knowing we can't have
it all,

We were still the son and a daughter,

Keepers of trust and hopes of our parents.

We followed the path chosen by our destiny,

Without fighting for each other even for once,

Not knowing if we will ever meet again,

Our lives parted ways in miles and like forever.

With our friendship in my heart,

I adorned the love and trust we were in,

You were all by my side in times of peace and distress,

An anchor hidden at the depth of my heart.

Between forgetting and remembering you,

Life happened,

I lived each day one at a time,

Scaring if I will ever meet you again.

But one day fear was taken over,

And I surrendered to the urge of my heart,

Need to see you for one last time,

Memory whispered a blur blueprint of roads leading to
you.

I struggled with fading hopes,

Walked in prayers to find your whereabouts,

Rewinding the path we once walked together,

And then, finally reached a door that felt like you.

I lied and pretended to be someone I'm not,
My guilt was silenced by my longing,
Got some numbers and some missing heartbeats,
Dialed but it was not our time to connect.
Days, then weeks, then months passed,
Before I totally gave up,
We finally spoke to each other,
You sounded so eager on phone and then totally distant
when we met.
Once again you flew far away,
Our conversations tried to make up for decades,
We kept in touch in spite of distance,
Life kept happening at your end and mine till we met
again on that day.
Wrapped in each other's arms after years,
It felt like nothing has changed between you and me,
Hours passed and time kept knocking on the door to
leave,
It was time to say good bye finally.
Holding you made me feel alive again,
This time with the pinch of obsession,
I missed the thin line between reality and illusion,
I lost the separating boundaries of your life and mine.
You distanced yourself which made me anxious and
desperate,
A wild river of frightening emotions broke in me,
Violent waters submerged the shores too,

The fear of losing you again was choking.
Friendship that sheltered me through thick and thin,
Was slipping from my hands like sand,
Everything just seems to sink and shrink,
I was alive but had no sense of life anymore.
You were gone and lost,
You closed all possible ways,
My despair and anger were rude,
But I was helpless.
Tears dried,
I pretended as though you are my long-forgotten
memory,
Kept myself deliberately away from caress of your
remembrances,
But, honestly speaking, you are still my habit in peace
and distress.
A lot has flown down the bridge,
Time has healed me here and there,
I understand now how I scared you,
And why you chose to disconnect.
Today the story of River Ganga feels so relevant to me,
She once brutally flowed destroying everything that
came in her path,
Then Lord Shiva rested Her on His head,
Now she flows peacefully to pardon the sins of people on
earth.
Likewise, I was so hurt and angry,

But life has taught me to flow with the flow,
Universe has put me on the path of purpose,
To meet women, I can serve.
I learnt holding on can hurt but letting go can set us free,
Whenever I'm wandering through mountains and
valleys,
And walking at the shores of a saintly flowing river,
I find myself closer to my soul.
Whenever pages recite poetries of friendship and love,
Yes, I still remember you very fondly every time,
I hope you will be able to forgive me,
I pray you live in Divine bliss.
I don't know if I will ever see you again,
Because I don't know if I wish to,
However, I wonder, will we pass as strangers with
grudges in mind,
Or will smile at each other understanding from where
we both come from.
I lost not only friend but my only love too,
A void resides in a broken heart,
Like deep scar of open wounds,
I don't know if I can ever make you understand this.
I was despairing to find a closure,
In ways my mind desires,
But life happens at its own pace,
And one fine morning memories didn't haunt anymore.
I learnt that closure is not something tangible,

Like pain and happiness, it too is a feeling,
I still have the pearl,
But it doesn't define my desires today.
I just lived million years in a moment,
Composing tender tale of memoirs of,
The flowers, the fragrance, the book, the pages,
And you and me.

2. Sensuality is no Shame, Dear Woman!

Adolescence blossoms,
And girl is no more a child.
She has a striking mind,
And her spirit free and wild.

Body revealing the secrets,
Of salient intense desire.
Innocence giving its way,
To lure overwhelming fire.

Beautiful, she feels within,
Sensuous in her bare skin.
No more a closed shy bud,
A flower she is; whole & keen.

If ever refuse to shame herself,
She is reduced as loud & vulgar,
Few surrender though unwillingly,
But some never silent their vigour.

When length of a cloth defines her,
She is judged and disgustingly touched.
A girl dies every moment thereafter,

Woman's humble soul forever clutched.

Some demons wound her modesty,
With dirty eyes, hands and thrust.
Some in name of obvious patriarchy,
Push her back to earth's crust.

Sensuality is not lust and sex,
It lies beyond her nakedness.
It's furious ablaze in her rebel,
And in gift to nurture tenderness.

In enraged waves of Wild Ocean,
Sometimes like smoothing moon light.
Into disastrously blowing winds,
Serene love becomes sensual knight.

Sensuality is in her resolute gaze,
A ravishing rising sun on horizon.
She is a revolution in herself,
When truly awaken and completely arisen.

Dare you mistaken her sensuality,
To intact virginity or ageing wrinkles.
She forgives to heal after every pain,
Hope in her quite eyes forever twinkles.

Inherited sacrifice from the origin,
Commitment is her pure sensuality.
Her strength to hold on and let go,
The womanhood is sheer tranquility.

She is the flow and flame on Earth,
Cherishing the Universe with grace,
Destined to be a nurturer,
Embracing the Divine with elegance.

She is not a woman of mere appearance,
She reflects strength and substance,
Alter your own acceptance, dear woman,
The spirit of nature resides in your existence.
Sensuality is no shame, Dear Woman!

3. Liberate

Fire from the radiating Sun,
Tinted splendid sky so bright,
Clouds in blues and whites,
Painted all with His fuming light.

Some hues scattered on this earth,
Unfolding magic of sinuous breeze,
Waters reflecting the sky above,
These sunny tones sprinkled at ease.

Somewhere near the shore of a stream,
Bundle of flames roared at mid noon,
Girls from bonfire are out here to rejoice,
To shed their calming pretends of moon.

The faraway landscape is sheer ecstasy,
They liberate from their remnants of sorrow,
And discard the obligations of womanhood,
Of yester years and of imminent tomorrow.

Long hair lay loose on their naked backs,
Hurling cloths of disgrace to soar with wind,
Their bare bodies now swinging to new rhythm,
The miraculous flares burnt melancholy in hind.

Sensuous souls bathed in deep violet waters,
Alluring the world with their youthful quests,
Rising on the waves of their eloquent spirits,
Gazed salient horizons with unfathomable requests.

Their love and friendship, they said, will last till eternity,
Thoughts embedded profoundly in the realms of their
souls,
Naive hearts rejuvenated in newly found comradeships,
Womanhood is embracing these girls with absolute
consoles.

Transformed energies and evolved synergies,
Girls broke the confinements of biased judgements,
They promised to hold each other in love and light,
Not in competition but in life long commitments.

Celebrate triumph and liberate in menace,
Girls raised the slogans loud and clear,
Above false envy and despair,
Let us bond to love and cheer.

4. When I More Often.....

When I cleanse myself more often than venting,
When I let go more often than holding on,
When I forgive more often than blaming,
When I pray more often than complaining,
When I sail on hopes more often than sinking in my own thoughts,
When I let patience protect me more often than anxiety misleads,
When I allow faith to guard me more often than trusting shallow motives,
When I release the gone more often than clinging to the loss,
When I accept unconditionally more often than judging,
When I surrender more often than controlling,
When I evolve in acceptance more often than denying the change,
When I kneel down to God more often than to situations,
When I go silent more often than reciprocating to chaos,
When I listen to the whispers of my heart more often than the noises around,
When I travel inward for guidance more often than reacting to outward opinions,
When I let purpose lead me more often than following the superficial confusion,

When I befriend myself more often than belittling
myself,
When I search for my soul more often than validations
from others,
When I let light of Divine guide me more often than
falling for the darkness of doubts,
When I let love of Universe guard me more often than
being distressed form hatreds,
Then I'm there where I'm supposed to be!

5. She: The Poem

She is a poem....
In the cries of her first lively breathes,
In the dimples of her sparkling giggles,
In the touch of her tiny hands,
In the twinkle of her cheerful eyes,
In the smile of her innocent face,
In the steps of her baby feet,
In the words of her joyful voice,
In the mischiefs of her playful heart.

She is poetic ....
In the dreams of her growing years,
In the adventure of her wild soul,
In the glances of her fierce rawness,
In the faith of her everlasting friendships,
In the prayers of her forever love.

She still echoes poetry...
In the tales of her blue heartbreaks,
In the shame of her miserable pains,
In the silence of her thrashed screams,
In the scars of her unhealed wounds,
In the betrayal of her trusted alliance,
In the rejection of her honest efforts,

In the tears of her scattered soul.

A woman is more than a poetry....
In the victory of her guilt battles,
In the acceptance of her sacred solitude,
In the rhythm of her wandering soul,
In the passion of her newly found life,
In the prayers of her divine rejuvenation,
In the strength of her believing miracles,
In the serenity of her vulnerable emotions,
In the energy of her driving lives,
In the blessings of her to the world.

6. Gypsy Soul

Slow and gentle was my pace,
Modesty was the feminine grace.
I was trapped in the version of normalcy,
And confined in the ideas of decency.

There was relentless deep inside,
Void and despair alongside,
But one day I whispered to humble me,
To seek adventures of mountain and sea.

She felt the energies of rising moon,
Tides and waves were symphonic soon,
Showed her fiercely flowing waters,
And liberty of nature that matters.

In the quest of enchanted desires,
Humble me just blazed into fires,
Invoking her soul of a gypsy,
Breathing the vein of ecstasy.

The birds rang the morning alarms,
Songs from forest were the new charms,
She walks on the path paved by winds,
And wanders to collect her precious gifts.

She states stories of spirited womenfolk,
And chant tales of indigenous folklores,
The photographs narrate her escapades,
Her passion to seek life is in festive parades.

Minimalism is her new sufficient,
Union with herself the quotient,
Inspired by simplicity of love,
Now not in love but she is love.

No anguish or anger in her heart,
She is learning the self-healing art,
Practiced by the women from the ancient,
Vintage wisdom translated in the present.

The gypsy soul has found the way,
Fairy in her spirits is here to stay,
The heart is hippie in every sense,
She is here to heal and cleanse.

7. Inheritance

I sat with the women of past and future,
Listening to the stories of their inheritance.
Some carried the baggage of humiliation,
Some burden of many betrayals.

One had scars from falling deep in the failures,
For another, the wounds from many battles were still
bleeding,
There, she hides her bruises from judgements,
Here, one heart is heavy with pain of negligence.

A friend waited too long for validations,
One desired for unconditional acceptance,
She was sold at a tender age,
Another raped for mere pleasure.

Women cried their hearts out for self and the other,
They can't measure the pain each one endured,
The young girls are scared to be women,
Will they too inherit the similar kind of fate?

One stood strong and fierce among all,
She was here to challenge the chronicle of womanhood,
Her questions deep rooted inside every heart,

"How many of you have hurt the other women?"

All were silent to reflect their conduct,
Have they behaved inhumanly with other women?
Who is responsible to malign the tribe of the supreme
nurturer?
The answers shook their own identities,

One was jealous of her own sister,
Other assassinated the character of her female coworker.
She ill-treated another girl to live in lust and lure,
To possess power, she brutally ruined few of us.

The gossips were at the forefront,
A sword to kill the moral of a fighting spirit,
Words can hurt or heal,
We knew but forgot to remember.

Quite were all and deeply thinking unanimously,
If we had chosen courage to stand for each other,
And not the fear of competitiveness amoung us,
Our lives would have been a tale of pride and
authenticity.

No judgements or blame game,
We all were on the same side,
Now its time to empower each other,

With kind words of love and empathy.

From journeys of desolation,
To triumph of unions,
We travelled miles as women,
Promising end of misery from each other.

We also spoke of men,
Their love and atrocities,
But they are less than half of a problem,
If we women stand together in thick and thin.

Holding hands to cross the cursed threshold,
Relinquishing and enchanting,
We women sang and danced,
Forgiving all within and out.

We women are guarded by love of Divine,
Guided by light of the Universe,
We pledge to purify our possessions,
For future women to inherit the virtues of divinity from
the past women.

8. The Moon

Sitting by the window,
I saw a lingering shadow.
A smile spread on my face,
As moon bestowed the grace.

Still in caress of my solitude,
I bowed with loving gratitude.
The moon is here to heal,
As he listens what I feel.

I speak in whisper,
And he is the keeper.
Friendship so pure,
Between us is for sure.

I shared my reminiscences,
And all your remembrances.
Distance between us is in miles,
But moon can see you in smiles.

Moon tales your peace,
Worry in my heart cease.
Moon listens to my prayers,
And knows all my cares.

My heart is the memoir,
Your memory a souvenir.
My longing for you is habitual,
Moon transcends it into spiritual.

As I evolve every night,
My heart illumed by moon light.
I found the solace,
And some romance.

From ache in despair,
To love that is rare.
Not a zeal of fantasy,
You are my sheer ecstasy.

Wrapped in your embrace,
I laid in the fragrance,
That moon lavishly sprinkled on me,
From the drops he brought from your sea.

9. Expression of Love

Some words on paper,
Scattered here and there,
I'm trying to search a story,
That ends happily ever after.
My words can never describe you,
Because you are beyond them for me,
Yet, I want to write you in hundred ways,
And read a million times to myself and you.
The papers are lying all around me in wonder,
These little secrets of romance are not aliens to us,
They said to me in whispers and recited words of you,
Together we wrote love stories that are blissful and real.

Some colours I chose,
To paint you on the canvas,
Should I begin with a rainbow,
Or spread of an autumn morning?
Colours saw my muddles and giggled,
Is he really every warm colour you chose?
They asked me in awe and waited for my reply,
I showed them hues and shades of our vibrant love.
Colours fused and decorated canvas like never before,
Stunned with every stroke & colour we chose for portrait,

You came walking through the meadows of beautiful
flowers,
Together we painted the ecstasy in serene colours of a
rainbow.

Words and colours,
I chose to express love,
I, not the master of either,
Have a heart that beats for you.
Rhythmic music for a soulful dance,
Or surreal poetry for captivated heart,
The waves of tranquilly flowing seawaters,
Or mesmerizing echoes of melodious countryside.
I can smell you in every scent of the sedative breeze,
I find you in illuminous moon light and dazzling
sunshine,
There's you in every twinkle of the spellbound banquet
of stars,
Love stories are found everywhere but ours in
togetherness forever.

10. The Monk

The question 'why me?',
Was led by many discontents,
In me and all around.
Dread in my heart,
Desolation within my bones,
Imbued pain had no sound.

The mystery called life,
Was plunging into deep valley,
Of despair and agony.
I was desperate,
To fly high on the wings of hope,
But was tied in monotony.

Intimidating life,
Hostile in my theories,
I desired for freedom.
And one day I stepped,
Onto the journey of revelations,
Authentic and random.

Seeking meaning,
And purpose I wandered,
Till I met a monk.

Serene he was,
In his simplicity and solitude,
Held me before I sunk.

"Chaos or silence,
Is a choice we make,
Every moment.
Beacons lie within,
Our awakened souls",
That's what he meant.

Grasped little,
But keen to learn more,
About conscious.
Habitations,
Of my perpetual soul,
Are now eternally joyous.

Surrender,
Is the only word he emphasized,
In Faith and in Divinity.
Salvation will come,
Practice Dhyan Sadhana and Samadhi,
The Supreme Trinity

11. Leisure

Leisure is so rare,
And springs in silence,
When mind is at ease,
And life seems to be simple,
As there is no eagerness,
But tranquil calm.

Leisure is in pages of old book,
Read a hundred times,
Over the last sip of coffee,
From the favourite mug,
The fragrance lingers,
Of coffee, the pages and the petals.

Leisure is to learn from the birds,
Surreal melody that hints the heart,
To beat in rhythm of life,
And the butterflies,
Hiding in the shrubberies,
Flaking the old-self for the new wings.

Leisure is watching the sun,
Rising on the horizon,
Colouring the sky in shades of red,

And then setting,
Behind the mountains,
Making way for the moon.

Leisure is to see the moon,
Hidden behind the clouds,
Yet whirling the ocean into tides,
And that spread of stars,
Bright and vibrant,
Sparkling like diamonds.

Leisure is solitude,
Sitting on the banks of flowing waters,
Or walking into the deep forests,
Tall treks on the mountains,
Found in profound caves,
And at the doorstep of spirituality.

Leisure is being myself,
With no strings attached,
And far from judgements,
When body is draped in strength,
My heart is filled with love,
And the soul that sees eternity.

12. Bucket List

I made a bucket list yesterday,
To live life before I leave this world,
There was so much to explore,
 I let my forgotten wishes unfold.

I want to buy a Barbie,
Tall, lean and with black hair,
Buy a dream catcher in white,
And put them together in pair.

Ink sun and moon,
On my collar bone,
Wear gypsy bangles,
'Coz hippie soul I borne.

I want to travel far and solo,
Making friends with strangers,
Sitting by the camp fire,
And listening to the story tellers.

I want to meet teenagers,
To know their aspirations,
Take a chance to see,
And speak to my inspirations.

Talk about fast fashion,
And pollution it carries,
Love people and planet,
For future with less worries.

Visit places of heroic legacy,
From the records in my diaries.
Meet the humanitarians,
Who selflessly leads charities.

My wishes are childlike,
And mature at the same time,
I have lost some in between,
But now everything seems fine.

I don't want to stop here,
By only penning my desires,
I want to live every word,
Like holding stars and sapphires.

Clock is ticking,
And so is my age,
Before I lose forte,
I want to leave the cage.

I want to go out in this world,

And make it a better place,
For generations to come,
May it remains a jubilant space.

Pages of my memoirs,
Are to inscribe victories,
Struggles and sacrifices,
Besides my bucket list stories.

13. Virtual Reality

Isolation is the new hype,
Distant the new genre,
Virtual reality the trend,
Where are we heading as a society?

Befriending strangers online,
Expressing the exasperation there,
Caught in the vicious cycle of triggers,
Is the beast of victimization longing for sympathy
virtually?

Influencers dominating the domain,
'Like, share and subscribe', they say,
From youngsters to aged are following,
Is social media driving our lives meticulously?

Posts on handles are to voice biased opinions,
Whether sensational, sensual or sentimental,
Laden with unjustified adulations sometimes,
Where are authentic and ardent creators of contents?

For the propagators of perpetual fiasco,
The thumbnail rule is to be viral,
Above morality and ethical values,

Aren't the using platforms to feed nonsensical lies?

These cybernetic proficiencies,
Can tarnish a character,
Or make lies popular,
Has it become the tool to build or degrade the
generation?

The reporting of community bashing agendas,
And flaunting political propagandas,
Donning the feather of paparazzi,
In-between where is that trustworthy correspondent
lost?

The seasons of web series that run endlessly on channels
today,
Have made audiences the onlookers of disheartening
stunts,
Of foul language, use of substance, violence and
vulgarity,
Is there any possibility to restore the innocence we once
watched?

The content creators are paid in lakhs,
To hook the youth online,
The reels, the videos and the contents,
Is it not riotous enough to make minds dormant?

Dark humour is the facet of filthy content,
Normalizing the bullying of naïve is tickling,
The myths surrounded around reality shows,
Why the sense of entertainment has deteriorated?

Great contents of history and geography,
And of mystic heritage and spirituality,
Are overshadowed by crude voices,
Why don't all have ethical backbone of morality and
responsibility?

Some souls have pledged to craft the lives of society,
With sustainable life skills and humanly behaviours,
To transcend into devoutness for people and planet,
And doesn't that sound like pinnacle of a civilization
ever dreamt?

14. The Healing

There I sat all by myself,
Lost in baggage of pain,
Eager to console myself,
I cried my heart in vain.

I held my aching head,
Desperate to breathe,
Chaos still in my head,
Trying to find my ease.

Need to stand now,
And get out of here,
It is never if not now,
Before too late to bear.

I walked for a mile,
On a path untrodden,
Hope seemed far a mile,
Felt weary all of a sudden.

I leaned on a firm rock,
For strength n' compassion,
The enormousness of rock,
Bursting with love n' passion.

It held my hand gently,
And showed me the woods,
I walked slowly and gently,
In the forests of leafy hoods.

Forest led me to the sinuous waters,
Flowing deep like mystic wonders,
Looking at the waves on waters,
My mind now ecstatically wanders.

'Help me heal' I urged,
'And take away my worry',
'Flow with the flow' she urged,
'Life is to live and not to carry'.

Don't burden yourself,
With regrets and guilts,
Don't anguish yourself,
And lie under dismay quilts.

I listened to all in awe,
And desired to inherit her grace,
I will walk back today in awe,
Carry all within me in fond embrace.

The calm and restoring streams,

Flowing down to seas and rivers,
May my thoughts become streams,
And tide into the oceans of forgivers.

Waters told me to pause and grasp,
'There's much more to calm pools,
I have layers to show and you to grasp,
Known as hurricanes and whirlpools.

I dive into the depths of water,
To find zeal and wilderness,
I carry within the same water,
Of forsaken and tenderness.

I learnt the vibrant lessons,
Of what to hold on,
When to let go lessons,
And how to move on.

My love is what I need,
To heal from my grief,
My soul is what I need,
To be my home of relief.

15. The Holy Dip

I have grown in lands of Bharat,
Where the landscape is wide-ranging,
To mention the scared forests,
And divine flowing rivers,
Banquet of high mountains and deep valleys,
And hometowns of revered Gods.

I witness the spiritual inheritance,
By devotedly participating in rituals,
Embrace traditional values with pride,
Witness planetary unions with poise,
And celebrating vibrant festivities with delight,
Also pray for ancestors' far and further journeys.

Born in the era of once in many lifetimes,
Blessed to experience the phenomenal,
Maha Kumbh at the Triveni Sangam,
An alignment of spiritual vibes on this earth,
When celestial Ganga meets sacred Yamuna,
And mystic Saraswati.

Millions of people gathered at the banks,
From my country and from abroad,
Congregation beyond caste, creed and religion,

And of elite, famous, ordinary or lost,
Unveiling the universal allure of spiritual legacy,
Bharat is recognized globally for.

The sacred pilgrimage fascinates millions,
But some managed to reach travelling endlessly,
To take a dip in holy waters,
And surrender oneself to the mothers,
Praying to cleanse and heal the past and future,
And to generously bless our present.

Watching the flood of people on all routes,
I was scared to step out and go,
But my heart was around the banks,
Waiting for my body to unite,
And one day I flew,
To rejoice with my heart.

Maha Kumbh encapsulates science,
And spirituality at the same time,
Ritualistic traditions, richness of knowledge,
The intrinsic practices and customs,
Of socio-cultural diversity at one place,
Can happen only in Bharat.

The calm in chaos was unbelievable,
The chanting stirred devotional vibrations,

The frequencies of universe were in sync,
With my mind, body and soul aligned,
This spiritual journey is mysterious and epic,
Every dip in holy waters transformed my energies.

Bharat is land of evolution,
Of many saints and hermits,
Preaching the religion of spirituality,
And teaching righteous walks of life,
Leading us to the virtues of God,
In one and many ways.

16. The Unconventional Woman

Prose and poems on unconventional woman,
Talks about her authenticity and confidence,
Words emanate the vibes of rebel and revolt,
And praises her curiosity and compassion.

Beautiful she is in her own uniqueness,
And alluring in her spirited aesthetics,
Unapologetically true to herself and all,
And reminds being oneself is enough.

Radiating vibrance in her aura,
She is guided in the direction of purpose,
Driven wholeheartedly and sincerely towards,
Discovering forever her own personality.

She is in the spotlight for her voices,
Encouraging and inspiring one and many,
Impacting the evolution of tomorrow,
By resolutely standing on her grounds today.

Fueled with the strength to embrace,
Vulnerability, not as her imperfection,
But as a stout weapon to console,

Support and uplift the distressed.

She does not gossip,
Nor malign any character,
She may be opiniated,
But indeed, less judgmental.

Her soul longs for new experiences,
Travels exploring people and places,
Voyages seeking adventures and thrills,
Learns and grows to unfold life itself.

Her curious mind and open heart,
Focuses more on resolution than trials,
Not oblivious to challenges or setbacks,
But her resilience is about sheer thriving.

She adapts, endures and survives,
Letting not adversity define her,
She emits optimistic energies,
And only gratitude refines her.

She leads by the example of inspiration,
Encouraging one and all to chase their dreams,
Leaning into qualities that make her,
Unforgettable, dependable and relatable.

Believes in nurturing real connections,
Built on trust and meaningfulness,
Enliven with deep conversations,
She gracefully listens, sees and values.

Every woman reflects the traits of Divine,
Unveiled in some and buried in others,
Nevertheless, she is a woman of substance.
She is an undoubtedly unconventional woman.

17. Manifestation

Holding gently,
I see through the Blueprint of my life,
Wondering where I am and where I want to be,
Should I let everything be; without complaints,
Or believe that all will be as I desire them to be.

Seeking answers,
I started wandering within me and around,
With intentions to find meaning to my existence,
I, with all my heart, reached the ever-guiding Universe,
She embraced my confusions with love and assurance.

Pronouncing guidelines,
She spoke about wishes and their manifestations,
Voiced the power of earnest belief and my resolve,
Universe will conspire and align with every reality,
She said softly, 'trust the process and slowly evolve'.

Listening carefully,
I envisaged my vigorous physique,
Restoring poise and strength within and out,
Activate the infinite power of my belief,
That I am eternally slender and stout.

Pointing gently,
She told me to be mindful of my self-worth,
Life will validate and world will fine-tune,
Believe in your potential to act and attract,
And live like the vivacious radiance of fortune.

Moving ahead,
She pointed the countless opportunities,
In the direction of my success and prosperity,
I just need to reposition my frequencies,
And manifest all I desire with integrity.

Adding further,
You may find home sometimes in a person or a place,
And may walk through woods for pleasure and peace,
But don't forget to come back to yourself often, my dear,
Remember within you lies all secrets of love and ease.

Slowing little,
She whispered about the magic of love,
Cherished harmonies and absolute intimacy,
The deepest connection that forever thrives,
I deserve the experience that embodies ecstasy.

Reminding me,
Resilience is my surreptitious strength,
Clarity unfolds as I intent to face every obstacle,

Trust and wisdom will guide me to transform,
Life into a resolute and eloquent miracle.

Diving deep,
Resonate in spiritual practices,
Connect to the divine wisdom,
Find moments of serenity and sanity,
Live in the spirit of freedom.

Preparing me,
She consciously reflected on a thankful heart,
Gratitude is the only way to abundance,
Where I am and where I want to be,
Universe manifests whenever I seek guidance.

18. Solitary Journey

Lonely or alone?
The question always lingers,
Like a meandering path,
Endlessly in my mind,
Leading to nowhere,
But chaos.

Lonely or alone?
I asked my heart,
Where to go,
And find answers,
How to be,
And with whom?

Lonely or alone?
The heart wondered,
And whispered to me,
To ask the flowing river,
The shining sun,
And the tranquil moon.

Lonely or alone?
I asked the river,
Mystically flowing,

In the woods,
With sparkling ripples,
She streamed into the ocean.

Lonely or alone?
I looked into the sun,
With each glimpse,
Of his supreme light,
He blessed solace,
To earth and living.

Lonely or alone?
I went to the moon,
When he illuminates,
The sky at night,
Revealed reliance on sun,
Thus, ascends and descends.

Lonely or alone?
I questioned a traveller,
Trying to find solitude,
Miles away from all,
Silently he claimed,
The path of self-discovery.

Lonely or alone?
I searched in a reader,

Unravelling the mysteries,
Of the extravagant world,
Quintessence of each word,
Was about the world in me.

Lonely or alone?
I studied from a hermit,
Solitary journey,
Reinforces essentials,
To pursue wisdom,
And find enlightenment.

Lonely or alone?
Is an unrequited search,
Into vulnerable complexities,
Drawn from the wavering mind,
Contemplating anguish of betrayal,
And brokenness of expectations.

Lonely or alone?
My heart said gently,
We are born alone,
And will leave alone,
We meet people in life,
For lessons to learn.

Lonely or alone?

The soul voiced,
We all are destined,
To encounter experiences,
Teaching what to hold on
And when to let go.

Lonely or alone?
Is no more a quest now,
I need to seek my own path,
Alive and enlightened,
Aligned with my soul,
Evolving and transcending.

Lonely or alone?
I told to my authentic self,
Is a spiritual journey,
To find oneself amid others,
Light lives on the way back home,
And finally merge into the divinity.

19. When I Finally Leave

When I finally leave from this worldly affair,
And walk back home climbing the heavenly stair,
I want to hold my breath and wait for a while,
To empty the baggage, I carry of flair and despair.

I tried to mediate on sounds and in silence,
Chose prudently my virtues of grace and elegance,
I lived my life experimenting and experiencing,
Its indeed a profound tale of calm and turbulence.

I want to sincerely forgive and seek forgiveness,
And mend if there is any kind of brokenness,
Let my heart now be empty of all grudges,
I lastly surrender to the absolute mindfulness.

With each step I let go of all judgements,
Vague promises and void agreements,
I don't want to carry burdens in my heart,
Of betrayals, enormity and foul sentiments.

My authentic self is holding mirrors for me to reflect,
This is the spell to trust heart more than the intellect,
Renounce everything that confines me in boundaries,
Either overwhelmed emotions or feelings of neglect.

Finally, this is the time to let you go forever,
My love, if not now then never,
The unfulfilled love still occupies my heart,
I leave with wishes to you for today and ever.

I pray to seek freedom from yearnings and memories,
To sanctify me with all pious and idyllic synergies,
I have released apiece of mine at every step upwards,
I now resonate frequencies of divine energies.

As I reached the alluring heaven,
I carried nothing of taken or given,
In awe I looked at my celestial Deity,
Enchanted marvels are seen and proven.

20. Mid Life Crisis

Ask me about mid-life crisis,
And just I ferociously rant,
About petulant discomfort,
Between my flesh and bones.

Chaotic they are,
The stages of menopause,
I wonder where will I belong,
Today and day after.

I lost metabolism,
And gained weight,
Sleep I tell you,
Plays hide n' seek.

My depraved appetite for food,
Humour and gatherings,
Is blamed to mood swings,
And raw reactions to hormones.

I don't look like before,
Nothing seems natural,
I behave strangely,
But what can I do?

I shout on kids,
Out of blue,
And cry randomly,
To get hold of myself.

Overwhelmed with love,
Feel entirely detached,
Both at the same time,
Like the lost and found game.

I count palpitations,
More than heartbeats,
My palms sweat,
And those hot flushes.

I'm on a roller coaster ride,
Adventurous as it can be,
My mind travels hundred miles,
Encapsulated in my bizarre body.

Depression knocking on the door,
Clinically proven deficiencies,
From medicines to meditation,
An effort to find lost grounds.

Women are prone,

And learn to cope,
All by themselves,
That's how it works.

Men live parallel lives,
To avoid confrontations,
Probably they don't know,
How to love and comfort.

The pain piles up,
Physical and emotional,
Children grow into their lives,
And men into their passions.

Friends are left behind,
And books don't console,
Where to go and whom to speak,
To find solace and ease?

Listen to discourses,
They suggest,
Will help little,
And give relief.

Will I ever heal,
From my ailing body,
That seized my mind,

And tarnished my repute?

I know it's part of life,
It shall pass too,
Giving me a new version,
For better not bitter.

As I wait eagerly,
To meet myself again,
I chose to live,
My mid life crisis ardently.

21. I, Me, My are Mine

On the final note written about me,
I want to be remembered as me,
Not as a daughter or a mother or a wife.
I tried to give my best as I lived,
But always fell short of something,
I can still say I had a wonderful life.

As a woman it was not easy,
To live all by myself,
No one to blame, it came naturally.
I chose my priorities,
Negotiating with me,
My life and me took decisions mutually.

I went missing in relationships,
Chosen or burdened,
Probably I was afraid of losing.
The other person,
More than myself,
So, I let go the privilege of choosing.

I submitted,
And let life happen,
With no interference as such.

I don't remember now,
What life summed up to,
Stable it was and me; as much.

I had no replies,
For judgements against me,
They argued if I am,
A victim or a culprit,
They gossiped,
Deciding who I am.

But universe had other plans,
Above me and my submissions,
It was rather unrealistic to unfold.
I was anxious,
But stability now suffocated me,
Transformed life was here to uphold.

I looked into the mirror,
And saw me as beautiful,
World beheld me,
The way I saw myself,
I became more aware,
Of my thoughts about me.

I stepped out,
To break the walls of confinements,

Built by me and my choices.
Rebel or revolt,
I don't want to define,
I raised above all such voices.

I reinstate my spark,
For myself and that woman,
Who struggles silently like I did.
Each battle is undeniably varied,
As every life of a woman,
We all need help to heal, indeed.

Finally packed my bags,
To travel lengths,
And breadths of my forgotten dreams.
Leading a purposeful life,
And adding meaning to each day,
While meeting women from all streams.

Filled with gratitude,
My heart reaches out to the universe,
Who held me in her compassion and caress,
Guided me with her radiant light,
And guarded with her caring love,
Gently revealing the secrets of life, she bares.

In whispers and signs,

Life unveiled the truth,
I, me, my needs my alike devotion,
To flourish and prosper,
Like my loved ones do,
Seeing self leads on to the path of evolution.

On the final day,
I am not the count of my deeds,
Or confined to my quests.
I am woman who lived,
An eloquent life,
To cosmos, I surrender my requests.

I'm a blessed soul,
'I, me, my' are all mine,
Now 'I' am seen,
I have 'me' time,
I lead 'my' life,
This is how I want to be seen.